REBUILD, FROM THE GROUND UP

From the Blueberry Field to the Boardroom

REBUILD, FROM THE GROUND UP

From the Blueberry Field to the Boardroom

by

REGGIE MOORE

ISBN: 978-1-7341717-9-2

First printing, 2019

Cover design by Prudence Makhuras
Book design & layout by Velin@Perseus-Design.com
Author Photo by Armon Dauphin

Manufactured in the United States of America

ABOUT THE AUTHOR

Reggie Moore is the Chief Executive Officer and President of Blue Cliff College. From Salisbury, Maryland, Reggie served in the Air Force for 15 years, and was promoted 14 times in 15 years working for Career Education Corporation before assuming his role at Blue Cliff College. With extensive background in operational and executive leadership, Reggie is passionate about uplifting others to their fullest potential, and will continue his mastery through a Senior leadership course at Harvard Business School. Reggie lives with his wife, Doreen, and takes great pride in his four children and five grandchildren.

To my wife, my family, and my friends.

CONTENTS

INTRODUCTION

I've experienced many things in my life. Although I'm currently the CEO and President of a higher education college, my life did not always seem so fortunate. In fact, I think one of the greatest dangers in observing someone else's success is thinking that you can't accomplish the same thing. Maybe you think that person had some predisposition for success, or everything went well for them along the way, and you won't succeed because you haven't been as lucky.

This is not true. No matter the circumstances into which you were born, your age, your gender, or your race, there is hope for you and your dreams.

I've had a lot of struggles in my life. If someone had looked at me as a boy, they likely would not have thought I'd amount to much. My life was not a lay-up. But I made the best of it, and I pushed beyond what even I thought possible. I knew that it didn't matter how big my problems were, so long as my relationship with God was bigger. My faith, and a few key lessons I learned along the way, were my pillars on this journey to success.

I want to share that journey with you, including how I went from working in a blueberry field to a boardroom. I may not have fit the statistics of someone who would one day grow into a CEO and President, but that didn't matter. I still knew I'd do whatever I could to make my dreams a reality, even if it meant rebuilding myself multiple times.

After sharing my story of building my life from the ground up, I'm also going to provide lessons for your career and life, including management tips and leadership tips that have helped me become successful. I even asked a few leaders I know and highly respect to share with you the most important lesson they ever learned. Some of these people I have worked for, some of these people I work with, and some of these people work or have worked for me. They have all experienced many things throughout their lives, and in this book, you will have access to their wisdom.

I have purposefully kept this book short. I think all great advice can be boiled down to a few key lessons, and the rest is up to you. The problem with reading self-improvement and leadership books is you can read all the books in the world, but if you don't go out and implement what you learned, what good are the lessons?

It's been a long journey, and I didn't always know if I would make it, but I'm glad to say that I'm happier and more successful than I ever thought I would be. I am going to share my story so that you know what's possible, give you the most helpful information I have gathered along the way, and then I want you to go out and implement what you've read, so that you can build a life beyond your dreams, too.

I hope these insights, stories, and suggestions inspire you to find the greatness that's already inside. As I take you from the blueberry field to the boardroom, I hope you will relish in the journey, and remember my favorite motto:

"Life is 10% what happens to you, 90% how you react to it."

No matter what happens—no matter how far you have to go—you can always rebuild yourself from the ground up!

CHAPTER ONE

EARLY LIFE

There are three memories that really stand out from my childhood and will help you understand where I came from.

The first is when I saw my dad throw a hatchet at my mom, intending to kill her while she was doing my cousin Marsha's hair. I was six or seven. That was also the day my mom packed me up, along with my three older sisters, and moved us to my grandmother's.

The second is I vividly remember going to a house called "Ms. Beulah's" to get secondhand shoes and wearing welfare glasses—the big-rimmed black ones that are now in style, but back then marked you as poor.

The third memory is being bussed to Prince Street Elementary and arriving as one of two black kids in the whole school. My teacher had me do a solo skit for a performance of some kind. I wore bib overalls, a straw hat, had a fake mule, and a song: "I got a mule, her name is Sal, 15 miles on the Erie Canal!"

There were some painful moments in my childhood. Even then, it was clear that if I was going to amount to something different than my upbringing, it would be my responsibility.

My journey of building and rebuilding myself from the ground up began here, with my foundation. Fortunately, there were some wonderful people in my family who taught me about hard work, giving back, and how to see my circumstances not as limitations, but as opportunities to grow.

The Importance of Family

My first role model was my mom. She was a hard-working mother. For all the years I can remember, she had two to three jobs. She went when she was sick, tired, and even when she didn't like her job in the least.

One of the worst jobs she ever had was counting strawberry plants. The room was cold and dusty. She and the other ladies sat on boxes and literally counted strawberry plants. It was horrible, and she probably made $80-$100 for an entire week's worth of work. When I was seven or eight, she sometimes took me along and sat me on a box while she counted. She even continued that job after I walked into the kitchen one day and discovered she was having a stroke. Everything she did was so that we could eat and would be taken care of. She made many sacrifices for her family, and she never once complained.

In the fourth grade, I learned from one of my classmates that my mom was their help. I was riding my bike home with Dicky T. He said, "Ms. Ina is your mom? I love her! She takes good care of my mom and dad and house." I hadn't known she did house work until then. When I heard Dicky say that, I didn't know how I felt about it. I was proud that my mom was a hard worker. Should I be embarrassed she was this family's help? It was confusing for a little boy.

From a young age, I saw that she was contributing to our family and giving us the best life possible. I knew I had a place in that, too. Each summer, from fourth grade through high school, I worked in the fields with migrant workers to pay for my school clothing and to earn my spending money. I remember there was something called a "Play Day" in elementary school where we could run races and win ribbons. In order to participate, you had to pay. I worked the fields so that I could pay to play.

We picked blueberries, strawberries, cucumbers, and watermelon, depending on the season. That was the start of developing a strong work ethic that would serve me for the rest of my life.

I would wake up at 4:30 or 5:00 a.m. and arrive at the fields which were still wet with the morning dew. "Migrant workers" at this time were African Americans from Florida who migrated around the country working in fields, following the crops that needed picking. My entire family went—my mom, sisters, and me. My two brothers were older and had already left the house.

The work was hard. Watermelon season was the worst. Up at 5:00 a.m., at the fields by 6:00 a.m., cutting watermelons till 3:00 p.m., loading them in a truck until 5:00 p.m., and then loading them into an 18-wheeler truck until 7:00 p.m.

I gave part of what I earned to my family. I knew the importance of contribution. The other portion, I saved. I was one of the only guys in my neighborhood who had money, and I had big plans. I truly hated being poor, and I hated seeing the other kids with their new bicycles while I rode a secondhand one. I even had tape around the nose of my thick-rimmed black glasses at one point—that was the poorest I ever looked!

I always had a sense that I was meant for something more. Working in the fields reinforced that for me, and it also gave me something I needed: the ability to work harder than anyone else.

Despite some challenging family situations, things weren't always bad. Some of the best times we had as a family was when we went crabbing in Maryland. We all went—my mom, dad, my three sisters, and my two brothers, including my brother Billy's wife and three children, and my sister Barbara's husband and their four boys. We were a large group, and one crabbing adventure in particular stands out in my mind as wonderful... and almost deadly!

I was about 10 years old, and the day started out as one of the best days of my life. If you aren't familiar with crabbing, here's how we did it: we tied a chicken neck to a string and submerged it in the water off a dock. When the crab took hold of the bait, we swooped in with a net and caught the crab. Later that night we'd cook them up for a delicious meal!

It wasn't the fanciest method—some people used crab traps instead—but it worked for us, and on this day in particular, we caught tons of crabs in a place called Red Hill, Virginia. As we packed up to leave, I ran back to get one of our nets left on the dock.

The net was stuck! No matter how hard I pulled, it wouldn't come free from the pole on the dock where it was caught. I yanked really hard, and, with a yelp, I was thrown into what I thought was the deep part of the water. I couldn't swim, and I was terrified.

What I didn't know was that, if I had stopped panicking, I could have stood. But blind terror had taken over, and I struggled with flailing arms and legs to get to the surface. I thought I was going to die. As my head dunked under three times, I did the only thing I could think to do: I prayed harder than I had ever prayed before. I knew God could save me, but I cried inside at the thought that he probably couldn't hear me all the way up there. Especially not when my words were garbled and watery!

As I went under the last time, I heard my brother Billy say, "Stop fighting, I've got you!" He pulled me out. There was water in my nose, my mouth, my eyes. I had swallowed so much, and I wasn't breathing. He gave me mouth-to-mouth, and I began to breathe again. He saved my life! To this day, Billy teases me about how hard I prayed with those garbled words that he heard across the dock. He can tease me all he likes— I'll forever be grateful to him!

Missing Male Role Models

When I was young, I struggled to have a positive, consistent male role model in my life. I really resented my dad. He was present for most of my other siblings' lives, and they really liked him, but after he tried to kill my mom, I only saw him occasionally. Worse, he lived with another family, and that lady had two sons. On Christmas, they got those new bikes I strongly desired. I knew he was my father, but for some reason he never felt like it.

Later in life I came to appreciate him. I learned that he did the best he could. He couldn't read or write and yet he was a truck driver! He would ask someone to make marks for him on a piece of paper, which he'd follow until the next stop. There, he would get new marks. At the time I didn't think he was very smart, but he must have been extremely bright to make his way from Maryland to New Jersey without the ability to read or write!

My father was mostly absent, and my older brothers were out of the house. But I knew I had a chance to be better than the men in my family, partly in thanks to my second role model: my Uncle Boyd. He was my aunt's husband, and I used to pretend he was my dad.

Uncle Boyd was always sharply dressed. I respected him for that, and I decided that if I looked sharply dressed, no one would be able to tell I was poor. So from grades 6-12, with the help of my sisters, I didn't look poor. I prided myself on being the best-dressed man in school, thanks to the example of my Uncle Boyd. I still couldn't invite anyone to my home, which would give our financial status away, but at least I looked good on the outside.

There's an old saying, "Fake it until you make it." And when I made it, I never changed my attitude towards dressing sharp. I pride myself on what I wear even now and how people see me today.

Naturally Gifted

No matter what I did, it always seemed like I was somehow different from my classmates. One day in elementary school my teacher said in front of the entire class, with the most Boston accent you could find, "I'm not used to being around a lot of blacks, but that Reggie boy, he's a smart boy." I remember thinking, "Wow." They may not have thought I felt racially discriminated against, but I did.

One thing that spoke louder than my being poor and black in an affluent, white school was I was very smart. In elementary school I got straight A's, except for art class. I refused to do a toothpick and glue structure for an art project. Mr. Hall, my Vice Principal, came and took away my patrol badge because my art teacher told everyone I got a D. I was so embarrassed. Anyone with a patrol badge was the big cheese, and now mine had been publicly stripped!

In junior high I played basketball, ran track, and discovered that I liked girls. And really liked the pretty ones. While making these discoveries, I also realized that I had to study a little, because other kids were smart too.

In eighth grade, I met a friend who changed my life. He turned me on to pot. I had tried it before, but when I smoked with him, I got delirious. Pot took away some of my ambition. My mom used to tell me, "Don't hang out with the neighborhood boys." So I didn't. I hung out with my affluent classmates, but what my mom didn't know was they were the ones who smoked a lot of bong and drank beer!

It was around this time that I started not wanting to be a nerd anymore. By then I had a "smart kid" reputation, so I started not trying as hard in school. I was dark skinned with big lips, welfare glasses, food stamps for my school lunches, and a bright reputation. The only way for me to really fit in with my peers became through pot and alcohol.

By the time I got to high school, I dated a few girls and even had my own car. It was a 1964 Ford Falcon from my dad with a dent in the door. With the gift, he also gave me some advice: never ride in the car with a bunch of guys. It wasn't a good look. But he said I could ride with as many girls as I wanted! I drove my girlfriend and her friends around. At then end of the night, they'd jokingly say, "Home, James!" I still smile thinking about it.

One area of school that taught me another valuable life lesson was athletics. Being successful at sports helped mold my competitive nature. I remember my track coach used to say, "Run a smart race. Be strategic." To me, he was saying, "Know who your competition is and use that to your advantage."

I have found this to be helpful in business and in life. It's okay to be a little humble, but be sure to kick some butt when your turn comes. I hate losing. Later in life, I knew that my secret to success would be that no one would out-work me, or out-practice me. I've always felt like I needed to be twice as good as everyone else to get the recognition I craved. And I mean craved!

My goal was to break out of the stereotypes into which I had been born. High school taught me that I liked girls and money, so the natural progression was to go to college and figure out a way to NOT be poor!

As it turned out, life had other plans in mind, but I knew one thing for certain: even though there were some aspects of my life I couldn't control, there was enough that I could. And if I chose to focus on the things I could control—and surround myself with smart people who could teach me what I didn't yet know—I knew I could reach any goal I set.

LEADERSHIP TIP BY GARY MCCULLOUGH

This is advice my father, a U.S. Army Sergeant Major, gave me, and advice I got from my first platoon sergeant when I was a brand new Army Lieutenant:

"Control your controllables."

Simply put, in the military, in business, and in life, there are things happening all around you all the time. It's easy to become distracted, confused, fearful, or overwhelmed by all of it. In order to slow things down, to make a plan, to ensure you give good direction to others, and to make good choices, it's important to focus on those things you can impact and to let go of those things you can't.

It's a simple reminder to be proactive and to not worry about the things you can't control.

When I am asked, "Why or how have you been successful?" I come back to **control your controllables***. When I walk into a room with five or seven or ten (or more) people, I know one thing for sure: I'm not the smartest person in the room. When I played sports, I was good, but I wasn't usually the best player. At a certain point, I couldn't influence those things. What I was able to control was how hard I worked and how hard I hustled. I controlled my controllables.*

- Gary McCullough,
Former CEO of Career Education Corporation

CHAPTER TWO

AIR FORCE AND COLLEGE

A Change of Direction

After finishing high school, my friends and I were hanging out one afternoon at the local playground talking about how badly we wanted to get out of town. They made a pact to go to the local army recruiter the next day, but I told them I wasn't going. I was going into the air force instead, which required a rigorous entrance exam.

To my shock, all four of them shipped out for the army the next day! Suddenly, our playground conversation became a reality.

I took and passed the air force entrance exam. Little did I know, I was about to start one of the most meaningful journeys of my life.

Air Force

I'm very proud of my fifteen years in the military. Going into the air force was prestigious. It gave me the strong foundation I needed to be successful later in life.

Like in school, I excelled in the air force. I graduated basic training with honors and was given my first assignment: air operations in "LA." *LA!* I soon discovered they meant "Louisiana."

One thing that really struck me about the military was they said everyone was blue. Not black, white, or brown, but blue. It was a way to make us equals, no matter our skin color. I really liked that, and it helped my self-esteem, given I had faced challenges because of my skin color up until that point.

In air operations, I scheduled flights for dignitaries— one-star Generals and up. This was another experience early on that boosted my self-esteem. The Generals always treated me like an equal, even though I was well below their rank. The culture of mutual respect taught me a lot, and was also different from my experiences growing up.

I made the next three promotions "below the zone," which means ahead of schedule. My pattern of success continued. I moved to recruiting, where I was rookie of the year, top high school recruiter, and top nurse recruiter. Two years in, I got to go back to Salisbury where I grew up. I remember people saying, "That's Reggie Moore. He made it!" I was making my own money, and I had prestige and acclaim. In short, I was fulfilling my vision for myself: that I could be more than a migrant worker in a field.

Another highlight from this time was being the MC for "Tops in Blue," a variety show in the air force. We traveled around with singers, comedians, and dancers, sort of like "Star Search." As the host, I also did a bit of comedy, sang, and introduced the acts. I loved it!

From recruiting, I was promoted to the processing center in DC where I was the youngest area training supervisor in history. At age 26 and 27, I helped train recruiters. This was a huge deal.

Finally, I was promoted to the recruiting services headquarters in San Antonio, Texas, where I greeted one-star Generals every day. It was like being a city councilman and working at the state capitol. It was a big move, and I was an exceptional staff member. No one really expected me to do so well, and I was glad to prove their expectations wrong.

But things weren't perfect, and my road to success was starting to get bumpy. Perched on top of the world, with a strong desire to be far more than average, I was about to fall hard, fast, and painfully. The question would be: after losing everything and feeling lower than I ever had, would I be willing to pay the price and once more work harder than everyone to attain the success I still craved?

LEADERSHIP TIP BY GARY CAMP

Everyone wants to be successful. No one starts out by saying, "I want to be average." Success in anything requires paying the price. Most people unfortunately don't pay the price and fall short.

– Gary Camp,
Former President and CEO of Premier Education

Challenges

Although I experienced great success in the air force, there were still some challenges.

Despite everyone being "blue," I had two dramatic racial encounters. This first one was in Louisiana. I went to buy a car, and another white guy wanted it. He threatened the person selling it and said to him, "I'm buying that car, you're not going to sell it to that nigger."

I was not used to that kind of racism. I remember calling my mom and telling her. She said, "You're in the south, you got to be careful."

In the second incident, a white man from Mississippi said, "Fuck you and the horse you rode in on." I didn't know what that meant, but we got in a fistfight. When we were reported, I didn't get in trouble, given what the man had said.

The other major challenge was of my own making.

My downfall was drugs and alcohol. Over time, my drinking and my usage got in the way of my ability to excel. It all came to a head when I was discharged. I was devastated, and as a result of my behavior, my first marriage crumbled.

I had married my first wife, Danita, who was a really sharp lady, and for the first 10 of our 14 years together, we enjoyed our DINK life—"Double Income No Kids." We lived in base housing without a mortgage, had cars, and other material items I only dreamed about as a kid. As far as I was concerned, I had made it, and my identity as "Officer Moore" was supposed to take me all the way into retirement.

It was over the course of those four years that things started sliding out of control until it hit a turning point I couldn't ignore. I was divorced, discharged, and my plans for my future were destroyed. At the height of my drug and alcohol usage, I couldn't see the way forward. I thought my life was over.

Things looked very dark. It wasn't until years later that I appreciated the power of this experience and how it shaped me.

I learned that truth is power.

We can't run from reality, and eventually, our habits and behaviors catch up with us. If I hadn't been honest and told the truth about my usage, I would not have gotten my act together, cleaned up, and found even greater success and happiness than what I had already accomplished.

Still, there was a long road ahead. Sitting at the bottom, feeling devastated, I knew I needed a way to rebuild myself, and there was only one direction I could go from here: up.

My Children

I haven't written about my children yet, even though they're the most important reason I've continued trying to be the best person I can be, despite the challenges I've faced along the way.

My oldest son is Reggie. He was a child I'd had with my high school sweetheart. We waited until we were

21, and Reggie was born four years after his mom and I graduated high school. Even then, I already thought I was destined for success, and if there is any good measure of whether or not I've accomplished my goal, you only have to look at my kids.

Reggie is an Information Technology Manager and extremely successful in his industry. My oldest daughter, Katrice, is the Vice President of a bank. My son Kyle just got his master's degree and works for a firm that's rebuilding the Golden Gate Bridge. And my youngest daughter, Sierra, just got her degree in Health Information, Billing, and Coding.

And that's to say nothing of my grandkids!

Sayla, my oldest granddaughter, is in her third year of college at LSU, and boy, is she smart! I am so proud of her. My other grandchildren range from ages three to eight, the youngest being Malaysia, then Adessa, then Milani, and my one and only grandson is the oldest, Miko. In large part, this book is a tribute to them, especially Miko, whom I think is going to be a world-famous soccer player.

Being a good dad has always been important to me. I'm very proud of my children, and I'm impressed by how they've all turned out, despite of their father! They are one of the main reasons I've been able to rebuild myself multiple times. And each time, in life and business, love was the key.

LEADERSHIP TIP BY LINCOLN FRANK

Don't leave love at the doorstep of business. All positive relationships—all great teams—are built on common respect, mission, and culture. The basic building block for that is love.

– Lincoln Frank,
Managing Partner for Quad Partners

CHAPTER THREE

NEW BEGINNINGS

If there's one thing I'd like to impart on you, it is that it's possible to struggle and still win. I've probably lived four lives in one lifetime. After being discharged, a new life was about to begin, including the journey into the field of education and being clean for over 22 years. I couldn't have accomplished any of it if it weren't for the people who mentored me along the way.

Mentors

I've been fortunate to have many mentors over the years, including people in my family, in the air force, and on the civilian side. These people helped me overcome the odds of growing up poor, with limited education and facing racial discrimination, and instilled in me valuable life lessons that made my success possible.

One of these mentors I met at age 35 when I started in education. His name was Dr. John Coover, but most people called him "Doc." He was the first one to tell me I could do something in business. He called me "Pup" because I was often the youngest person competing against candidates who were my senior. Thanks in part to his belief in me, I was promoted 14 times in 15 years in a company called Career Education Corporation, staring as a sales representative and ending as a Senior Vice President.

Those 15 years weren't always easy. I had just gotten married to my second wife, Doreen, and a week later, the company offered me another promotion, but I had to move to Portland, Oregon. We were living near Doreen's family in New Jersey, and I remember telling her that we needed to move to Portland. Her mother and family were not happy. Neither was she, for that matter. Given that we were newly married, I felt insecure making this request, but my wife supported me, and we made the move together. After we arrived and I started the new position, I heard my boss tell the CEO and founder of Career Education Corporation, Jack Larson, that he didn't know if I had the skillset to do the job. He questioned if they had made the right choice in moving me out there. I was devastated! I had just uprooted my new family, and now they doubted me!

But I hadn't come this far and overcome so much to quit. A different kind of mentorship saved me. Doreen went out and bought me a book called *The Power of Positive Thinking*. I knew I had a strong work ethic and I could do a good job, but now, armed with this book, I started working on my positive self-talk too. I needed to be my biggest champion and so mentally strong that no one could bring me down. Five years later, the guy who was my boss started working for me in a different division of the company.

As the saying goes, "Tough times don't last, but tough people do."

My greatest mentor of all was my former father-in-law, Wayne Wilson. He has been like a father to me, and is the man I respect most in this life. He's a true war hero—he was shot in the head in Vietnam, and now, 60 years later, is a Baptist minister.

When I was struggling with drugs and alcohol, he lost faith in me. I was no longer a good husband to his daughter, and I lost both his trust and my marriage at the height of my challenges. Later, he forgave me, and we now have a great relationship. In fact, one of the reasons I wanted to get clean was because I didn't want to keep losing people I cared about, like Wayne. He and others were my inspiration for turning my life around.

Wayne taught me three important things that guide me even today: Keep God first, take care of your body, and save your money.

I also learned that if I did what I always did, I'd get what I always got.

This meant that if I wanted to make changes in my life, I needed to address the very root of my behaviors and habits, working from the inside out!

LEADERSHIP TIP BY BASIL KATSAMAKIS

When someone at a meeting says, "We've always done it that way," I say, "Roast Beef." Everyone who has worked with me for a while knows what I mean. For the newbies, I tell them the following story:

At a holiday celebration, a newlywed is making the roast beef dinner. All the aunts, mother, and grandma are in the kitchen observing her preparing the roast beef for roasting. The newlywed puts on various spices and cuts three inches off one end of the roast beef and puts the bigger piece in a pan. All the women show their pride but one aunt asks why she cut off three inches. The newlywed replies, "Because mom did it that way." They turn to the mom and ask the same question. She replies, "Because grandma did it that way."

They ask, "So grandma, why did you cut off three inches?" In the corner grandma shakes her head and says, "BECAUSE IT WOULDN'T FIT IN THE PAN!"

That's my roast beef analogy!

– Basil Katsamakis,
Chief Operations Officer of Quad Partners

CEO

One of the hardest things I did was to step out on faith and leave my secure job working for Career Education Corporation (CEC)—which I had done for 15 years, starting after the military—to start working for Blue Cliff College as the CEO, where I am to this day.

When I was thinking about leaving CEC, I went on a tour in the south with a man named Basil Katsamakis. Basil was, and still is, the Chief Operations Officer for the overarching business that owns Blue Cliff College. We had a great time together, and I really respected Basil, but I initially turned down the position. I was not crazy about moving to the south to take the position. More than that, I wondered if I wanted to change directions after 15 years of success with one company. What would it be like to start something completely new? Could I manage being that far outside my comfort zone?

Fortunately for me, they did not accept my refusal. A week later I traveled to New York to meet with Basil once more, and three other gentlemen—Russ Dritz, Andy Kaplan, and Lincoln Frank—all of whom have changed my life for the better. They were a team. Like Basil, they all worked for the company that owned Blue Cliff College, and they were eager for me to take this job. Lincoln Frank was clearly in charge, and someone for whom I immediately felt great respect.

These three men seemed to be honest, direct, and driven. I could not help but be drawn to their energy, and to the great success they had achieved. Each looked me square in the eye as they shook my hand. I thought, "Boy, I'd like to be a part of what they are creating." On that trip, I felt committed to them and their vision.

Keep an eye out—you'll find leadership tips from two of these men in the book!

Still, I needed one final push. Changing my career felt like a huge step, and I wanted to be sure I had what it took to be successful when, in some ways, I was rebuilding myself again—not entirely from the ground up, but it felt just as new and frightening.

I found the help I needed in my mentor, Jack Larson. As previously mentioned, Jack was the CEO and founder of Career Education Corporation, the company I had worked for until then. Given his knowledge and expertise of what it took to be a CEO, I asked if he would come to my house so we could talk. He helped me ask all the right questions for this new job, and ultimately helped me learn that yes, I did want to try something new, and I was ready. I had worked so hard throughout my life to rise above my circumstances and challenges. Now, after all my trials and years climbing the ranks, I had a chance to achieve the penultimate experience for many working professionals—to become the CEO and President of a company.

Because I had gained so many tools over the years, I knew I could be successful in the role. Every single lesson I had learned brought me to this point, including the challenges I had faced with drugs and alcohol. Whether it was getting clean or working in the blueberry field, I had cultivated a hard work ethic. I knew that same hard work ethic would serve me well in the boardroom. I wanted to prove to others and myself that I didn't need to be the smartest person, to have come from wealth or privilege, or to have led a life without struggles in order to accomplish my dreams. Given all I had been through, if I could succeed, so could everyone else, including you.

Since working at Blue Cliff College, I have learned many valuable lessons. We offer a diverse range of degrees and training programs to make high-quality education accessible for all students. Our goal is to run the kind of college our sons, daughters, sisters, and brothers would be proud to attend. We treat all our employees with dignity and respect, and anyone who works at Blue Cliff College would say they feel proud to have any of their family members attend.

We like to say that we don't have second-class students, we have second-chance students. As someone who needed a few second chances, I can relate to where some of our students are coming from, and I am honored to be a part of a company that works to provide valuable education to those who might not otherwise get it.

Our work impacts people's lives, giving them another chance to train in the career they want to have, and our students' success stories are inspiring and humbling. I can't think of more fulfilling work, and it never would have happened if I hadn't leapt into the unknown. I knew that I had the chance to join a team working to change students' lives, and given how many people helped me along my journey, I feel blessed to at least try and return the favor.

LEADERSHIP TIP BY JON COOVER

Our success can only be measured by our continuing attention to our student value proposition. Keeping the promises made opens [the students'] window of opportunity to reach their dream. Nurturing them along their path shows we are focused on student outcomes and investor confidence. The surest way to make this happen is to be consistent and constantly communicate with each student, remembering: less is more.

– Jon "Doc" Coover, PhD

Loss, Love, and Faith

After my discharge, divorce, and even thoughts of suicide, I began rebuilding my life, which ultimately led to me being CEO and President of Blue Cliff College. My wife, Doreen, has been instrumental in it all. She loves me in ways I never thought possible, and I couldn't have clawed my way back to health and stability without her.

Shortly before our wedding, my sister Pat and my mother died. They were the two most influential women in my life. Both deaths greatly affected me, but I had Doreen's love and my faith in God to help me through.

Later, at the 10-year mark of being clean and sober, a second wave of deaths hit. My wife's father, her mother, and my oldest sister—who was like a mother to me— all died. Again, I was shaken to my core, and I had to lean on my wife for support, and my strong faith in God. Through these trials of the heart, I learned that I could survive my emotions and continue rebuilding my life even in the face of loss.

I realized struggles and hardships are unavoidable, and I wanted to find ways to grow through them and become stronger, rather than feel weakened by grief. After all, we grieve because we love.

Still, it's no wonder that after all of this happened, I was diagnosed with high blood pressure, high cholesterol, and borderline diabetes.

Again, it was time for some rebuilding.

I started eating right, exercising, and meditating more. My actions made a difference, and I felt empowered when I lost 30 pounds and came off the medication for high cholesterol, with no trace of diabetes. I still take medication for high blood pressure, because it's hereditary, and I know that prioritizing my health has increased my opportunity to live a full life. I want to live a long life so that I can be there for the people I love.

Building one's life from the ground up involves taking care of ourselves spiritually, mentally, and physically, so that we can continue to enjoy the delights we've worked so hard to attain. Then, we can spread that joy and gratitude to everyone else, and teach them that, no matter the cards they're dealt along the way, they, too, can create a wonderful life.

Your journey will also include hardships. We cannot avoid the deaths of loved ones, or when the market crashes, or if our company folds and we lose our job. Hardships don't only happen to some people; they find us all, eventually.

Craft your life in a way that allows you to stay resilient through your challenges. I mentioned two of my strongest resources: my wife and God. Building healthy relationships is critical to finding success—whether it is your relationship with yourself, the people you love, or with God or a higher power.

We can't do everything alone in life, and we shouldn't.

Invest in the people who matter to you. Support them when they need you, and lean on them when you need help. Cultivate a healthy mind, body, and spirit. Strengthen your faith in God and in yourself so that you know: when hardships strike, they might knock you down for a bit, but you have everything you need to get back up. It's important to take life one day at a time, and live each day to the fullest.

LEADERSHIP TIP BY STEVE FIRENG

"Wherever you are, be there."

I try to live by this quote in business and life. You have to be very intentional on where you are at that moment. Not to think about things outside that moment. This could be in a meeting, or watching your kids play soccer... be there!

– Steve Fireng, CEO Keypath Education

CHAPTER FOUR

LIFE LESSONS

I **think that life is 10% what happens to you and 90% how you react to it.**

You can fall short, but it's not okay to stay short. You have to get back up. There is no dress rehearsal for life. We only get one shot.

I've had my ups and downs. I've also had a lot of loss in my life, as I mentioned above, and they were deep losses. But I've survived the emotions, just as I've survived every other aspect of my life. And as long as I focus on how I react to my life, rather than what happens, I know I've got a healthy way to keep moving forward.

I also know that time is short, and we don't know how long we have. My wife and I owned a Pomeranian for

11 years. Suddenly, the dog became sick. We took it to the vet, who told us the dog had cancer and only two days left to live. We were devastated. We carried the dog up and down the stairs, nursed it, and cared for it. As it turned out, the dog lived another three months.

It got me thinking: How would we treat people we care about if we thought they had only two days left to live? I now look people in the eye a little more and think that this might be the last time I talk to them. You never know. Perhaps knowing we will all die is a good way to appreciate the things we have right now. Perhaps it is a good reason to be kind to ourselves, and believe in ourselves too!

When I was discharged from the air force, I thought my life was over. Once again, I had to rebuild myself, from the ground up, just as I had done to avoid a life working in the fields. Except this time, I felt like I'd fallen from the top, and it was painful. If I was going to find my way back up, I needed some new skills, perspectives, and life lessons. I knew I had to do some things differently.

LEADERSHIP TIP BY JAMES AMPS

"If you want something you've never had, do something you've never done."

Human instincts pull us into a direction of familiarity. We get used to doing something so we keep doing it, believing it keeps us in a comfort zone of no resistance. However, if you are going to go after something in your life you know is going to bring joy and possibly more peace of mind, you most definitely have to leave your comfort zone and do something out of the norm.

– James Amps,
Regional Director of Admissions at Blue Cliff College,
CEO and Founder of Amps International

Rebuilding

At age 40, I was starting a new career, getting a divorce, watching my mother age, and I had another child. It was a lot of change at once, but not all bad. My daughter is one of the joys of my life. And because life was now asking more of me, I was able to take better care of myself physically and psychologically. The new journey upon which I was embarking was both frightening and liberating. Some of my most valuable lessons came from being forced to rebuild my life from the ground up.

In spite of everything I faced, I persevered. When I joined Career Education Corporation, I started to believe in myself again. Through that belief and hard work, accolades and awards began to reflect my newfound success at a staggering rate.

- In 1998, I received the first ever Eagle award.
- In 1999, I received the Eagle award again.
- In 2000, I was recognized as Regional Director of the Year.
- In 2001, I received the Senior VP Leadership award in the category of Leadership.
- In 2002, I received the Senior VP Leadership award in the category of Exceptional Training and Leadership.
- In 2003, I received the prestigious Chairman's trophy, only awarded once a year.
- In 2005, I received Senior Executive of the Year as Senior VP of the company.
- In 2008, I joined Blue Cliff College as CEO.
- In 2013 and 2014, I was recognized as Top Executive of the Year.

The reason I did well wasn't because I was better than anyone else.

It was because I decided that, even if others had more talent or education than me, they would never out-work me.

I remember during my first job as a sales representative I vowed to make more phone calls than anyone. If I knew someone was making 50 calls, I would make 60. If they made 70, I would make 100! I would come in early and stay late. I wanted to be successful and I was willing to do whatever it took.

It's a little startling for me to list all my accomplishments out and reflect on my track record of success. Besides hard work, how did I do it? How did I come back from a devastating failure to become a respected, successful professional in a new field of work?

There are a few key tools I learned along the way that I'd like to share with you. Some relate specifically to business, and others can be applied to life in general. These lessons have been the cornerstones of my journey. I hope they will be of service to you as you pursue the life of your dreams!

Tools for Life and Business

Take everything one day at a time.

If you look at a mountain from the base, the hike to the top seems daunting. There have been plenty of days when I've felt low. Remember when my boss told the CEO that he didn't know if I could do the job I'd just been hired for? That was a low moment. But I knew I couldn't let it get to me. A few days later, after the initial sting wore off, I saw the opportunity this experience presented to me: I could grow in my internal strength. I felt motivated to work even harder and prove I was worthy of the job, and I also learned how positive affirmations could keep me mentally resilient.

Things might look bleak today, but don't fall into the trap of thinking that it will be bleak tomorrow, or the next day. Take things one day at a time, just like each step up the mountain, and before you know it, you'll have traveled a long way.

Find positive affirmations that work for you and repeat them over and over.

Positive affirmations are a great way to train your brain in the direction you want. We need to be conscious of our thoughts. Are they positive? Are we getting lost in blame and victimization? To help train my thoughts, and to feel grounded in how I want to live, I say these three positive affirmations every single day:

"If God be for me, who can be against me?"

"I can do all things through Jesus Christ, who strengthens me."

"This is the day that God hath made. I will be glad and rejoice in it."

Believing in God was a huge part of rebuilding my life from the ground up. When we feel low, it's helpful to rely on something larger than us—someone who can support us and believe in us—so that we can start believing in ourselves.

Find three positive affirmations that inspire you and say them every day. Even if you don't believe them right away, you will over time.

To love and be loved is crucial to success.

If we aren't able to give and receive love, what's the point of it all? Practice loving others and receiving their love. Invest in your relationships. They are the most important part of your life.

Don't be afraid.

Even if you've never done something before, try it. You don't know what you're capable of until you try. Before I started working for CEC, I didn't know I could work in education. Before I became CEO and President of Blue Cliff College, I didn't know if I would be successful in the role.

Things might seem scary, but once you start your journey, you'll learn that there's nothing to fear. And if you're the only one doing something, don't let that stop you. Do it anyway!

Always, always, always be on time.

I live by the Lombardi rule: always arrive 15 minutes early. It makes a great impression! Also, you can use that time to prepare yourself mentally and be in the moment, as Steve Fireng suggested in his Leadership Tip.

Treat your dreams with the respect they deserve, and demonstrate that you're willing to do whatever it takes to reach them, including being ahead of schedule.

Dress for the part you want.

As you know, I used clothes from a very early age to start embodying my dreams. When I was young, I didn't want to look poor, because I didn't want to be poor. That behavioral shift was the start of my journey of getting myself out of poverty!

I stick by this rule even today. The motto "dress to impress" goes beyond how other people perceive what you are wearing. If you dress for the part you want, you will start to act the part, too.

I don't care what everyone else does, but a shirt and tie has always worked for me!

Always keep a list.

My mentor Jack Larson taught me this. Go into each meeting or call with a list of things you want to accomplish, ask, or contribute. Do not be caught unprepared, or you will look as if you don't care. This is especially true if you're going to interview for a new job. Be prepared with questions and answers—show that you thought about things beforehand!

Stay focused.

We live in a world with endless distractions. You only need to go on the Internet or social media and an entire day can pass before you look up again. Whether it is in your daily work or planning yearly goals, never lose sight of what is important. Stay focused on your dreams, and work towards in every moment. Dreams don't come true on their own— they require dedication, and a willingness to set aside the distractions so that you can do what is most important to make progress.

Out-work everyone.

Hard work and commitment always win! As you know, I decided even when I was young that no one would ever out-work me. I don't care if I'm the smartest or not, because I know I'll always work the hardest, and no one can take that away from me. Don't let your insecurities about your intellect or talent get in the way of your dreams. Instead, train yourself to become a hard worker. Imagine everyone else as your competition— the way to win is to out-work them!

Work with intentionality

During my 15 years at CEC, a gentleman by the name of Gary McCullough became CEO. He was an amazing leader, and he taught me many things. Among them was to always work with intentionality.

What this means is to be specific about what you're doing and why you're doing it. Because of his advice, I now conduct every single meeting with intentionality. I start by asking my team, "What do we want to get out of this time together?" That way, we stay focused and we're all working towards the same goal.

You can apply this to your personal life and dreams, too. As you chart a path for your future, ask yourself: what are you doing, and why are you doing it? Your answers to those questions will give you a direction and help you create goals for your career.

When nervous about a meeting, take God in with you.

It is normal to feel nervous. Whether you are about to enter an important meeting, an interview, or a presentation, draw strength from something greater than yourself. God will support you and believe in you, even if you don't believe in yourself yet. If you want, you can even leave an empty chair beside you reserved for God. No one needs to know that he's silently there, giving you strength and courage.

Don't let success blind you to what's important.

My family has always supported me. My sister Hattie allowed me to live with her during one of my low points. I remember she told me, "I know you will get back on your feet, but when you do, don't be so uppity!"

She didn't know it at the time, or maybe she did, but this was a valuable management tip: "Don't buy your own commercial."

When you are doing well and people start recognizing and praising you, don't let it throw you off track. Sometimes the taste of success can turn into your

43

biggest barrier if you don't stay humble! Instead of getting distracted by your accomplishments, keep your head down and work even harder. The journey isn't over, so resolve to play the long game and stay focused.

This lesson helped me get promoted more than just one, but 14 times in 15 years. It was Hattie's love that helped me remember what was important: staying grounded, working towards my dreams, and the love and support of the people around me. Which leads me to my final tip:

You need good people.

As my mentor Jack Larson used to say, "Fish and loaves only works in the Bible." In other words, success in your business endeavor won't happen through a miracle. You need good people on your staff, and you need to invest in positive communication and a collective vision.

It's a well-known fact that you manage a process, but you lead people. To be a great leader, you have to be a great follower. Remember, you don't have to have all the answers, but you do have to be open-minded to the ideas of others.

Great leaders and managers are willing to do that one extra thing to go the extra mile and help people around them be successful. They work with passion, hard work, and humility. Finally, they treat their employees with respect and dignity.

These characteristics have helped me every step of the way.

LEADERSHIP TIP BY JOHN KING

Leaders create a vision and strategy to move the organization forward, assemble a competent team to achieve that goal, teach team members the skills necessary to maximize results, empower the team to take action, hold him or herself and the team accountable for those actions, and provide the motivation and resources necessary for success.

– John King Ed.D., Former Senior VP of Career Education Corporation, Founder John King EDD

Cultivating tools for a successful life and career are important because they give us a structure from which we can build. That structure supports us when we feel nervous or weak, and it lifts us up when our success is finally recognized. I hope these tools are valuable for you as you create the life and work you want. I can honestly say that they're all still working for me!

ANYTHING IS POSSIBLE

I want you to know that anything is possible, and there is always hope for you and your dreams, no matter how dire your circumstances might seem.

Life doesn't have to define you—you get to define your life.

But if you want your life to look different, as my friend James says, you need to *do* something different. Success doesn't happen without effort, and that effort is what makes your success all the sweeter.

I went from the blueberry field to the boardroom. For me, it took four things to succeed: hard work, perseverance, a belief in God, and humility.

I hope these stories and lessons have shown you that anyone can build the life they want—no matter how many times they have to rebuild—including you. As you go out into the world and implement these tools, I wish you all the best on your own journey of success!

ACKNOWLEDGMENTS

I have a lot of people who've helped me along the journey of my life, and I'd like to take the time to thank them.

To my long-time friends: James Amps, Tom Dashields, Broderick Nutter, Robert Broadwater, Ted Hill, Bo Clark, Donald Corbin, Thad Kittles, Mark Gortman, Barry Dennis, and Steve Fireng.

To my spiritual brothers: Michael Watts, Jerry Neal, Darryl Malden, Ruben Rabel, William Ross, Lee Osborn, Thomas Pointer, Aurthur Stevenson, and Benny Lee.

To my family: Sisters Hattie Laffeyette, Jacqueline Henley, and brother William D. Moore.

To my special nephew and best friend, Douglas King.

To my kids: Reggie Jr., Katrice Below, Kyle Riley, and Sierra Moore.

To my many nieces and nephew, and to my godchildren, Monte King, Sherell Henley, and Justin Dennis.

And to my wife, Doreen, the love of my life!!

Thank you all.